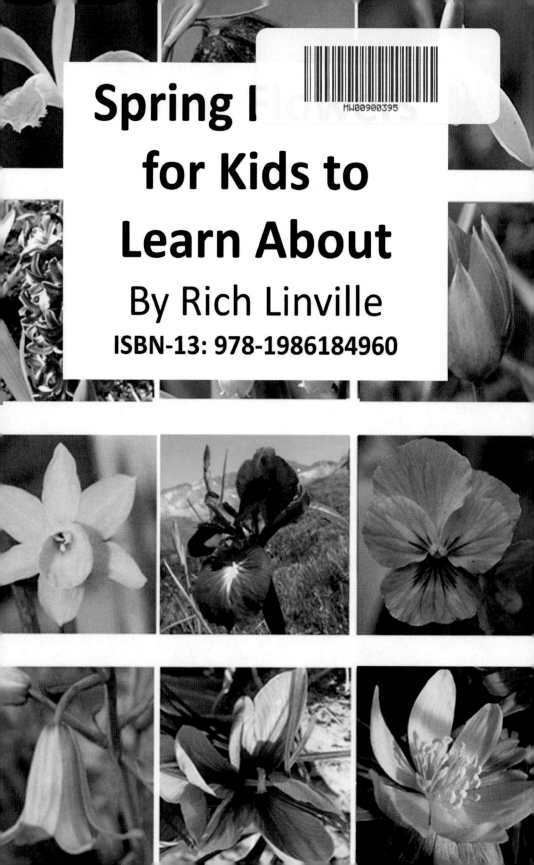

Spring Flowers for Kids to Learn About

By Rich Linville

ISBN-13: 978-1986184960

Even though they are called spring flowers, they can bloom at other times of the year in different places. Also, indoor and outdoor gardens can bloom at different times compared to flowers in nature. Find out from a local plant nursery your plant hardiness zone where you live to help you grow your flowers outdoors. Do not eat flowers, seeds or bulbs. Some are poisonous for protection.

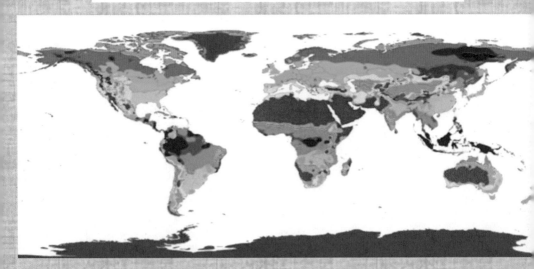

#1. What do you think this flower is called?

#1. In nature, blue flowers are difficult to find. This plant has many shades of blue and has a flower shaped like a bell. In a garden, if you add plant acid to your moist, well-drained soil, then the colors may become darker. This plant needs full or partial sun and grows best in zones 4 through 9. The color and shape of the flowers tells you that this is a Bluebell (BLOO-bel).

#2. What do you think this flower is called?

#2. This flower comes in many colors like pink, purple, yellow, orange, multicolored, and more. If you plant the bulbs in October, they usually spread and come back to bloom year after year. The pointed end of the bulb should be facing up. Plant the bulbs in groups in wire cages to keep animals from eating them. They grow best in zones 3 through 8. This flower is cup shaped and has very little or no smell.
It is a Crocus (KROH-kuhs).

#3. What do you think this flower is called?

#3. This flower has a trumpet-shaped center and is usually surrounded by six petals. It smells nice and can be pink, orange, yellow, white, two-colored, or three-colored. A natural chemical found in this plant may be helpful in treating brain cancer. But, this plant can be poisonous to you and your pets. This plant grows best in zones 3 through 8.
This is a Daffodil (DAFF-uh-dill).

#4. What do you think this flower is called?

#4. This plant has a group of flowers along the plant stem. Wear gloves when holding this plant's poisonous bulb that can irritate your skin. The waxy flowers can be red, orange, yellow, pink, blue or purple. When the flowers open, they look like tiny starfish. The flowers smell very nice. The planting zone is 4 through 8. Over the years, the flowers may bloom smaller and smaller. This plant is a Hyacinth (HIGH-uh-sinth).

#5. This flower is named after the Greek goddess of the rainbow because they have many different colors. But the most often color is purple. They are very simple to grow indoors or outdoors. They can grow in water or on land. They have 6 petals with 3 standing up in the middle and 3 falling away. This flower can grow in zones 3 through 9. This is an Iris (EYE-ris).

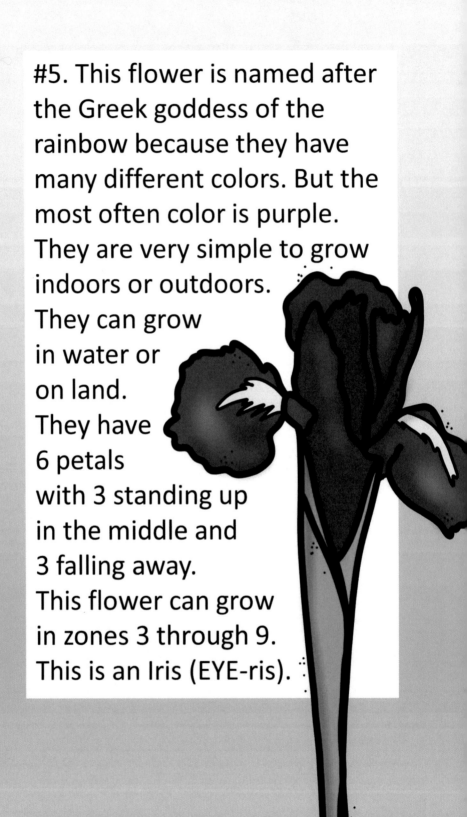

#6. What do you think this flower is called?

#6. This plant makes a spreading clump of large green leaves with short stems of white flowers shaped like bells. The plant spreads quickly. It is a favorite flower for growing as ground cover in shady places. The flower grows in zones 1 through 9. It grows well in tubs. This flower is Lily of the Valley (LIL-lee uv thuh VAL-lee).

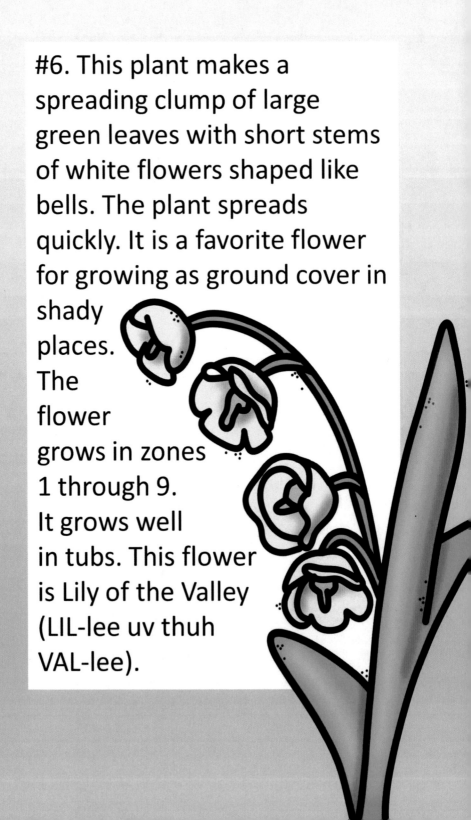

#7. What do you imagine that this flower is called?

#7. These are fast-growing, rounded flowers with five petals. They may be one color such as red, orange, yellow, white, blue, purple, and brown or many colors with black lines from the center. Some flowers have a dark center that look like a face. They can grow about 9 inches high and spread 12 inches wide. They grow best in zones 4 through 10. This flower is a Pansy (PAN-zee).

#8. What do you figure that this flower is called?

#8. This plant has a single folded leaf which may fall off before the plant flowers. The pink flower has a white edge that is marked with brown on the inner surface. This plant may be grown outside in a sheltered rock garden if the winter is not too cold. This flower grows best in zones 8 through 11. This is the Windowsill Orchid (WIN-dough-SILL OAR-kid).

#9. What could this flower be called?

#9. This flower has a spotted pattern in shades of purple, pink or pure white. It does a snakelike nodding of the flower on its long stem. It can grow in river meadows or the damp soil of grasslands. You can plant the bulb of this flower in a grassy area or under trees. It is very easy to care for and is slow growing, It grows best in zones 3 through 8. It is called Snakeshead (snayks-hed).

#10. What might this flower be called?

#10. This plant has two long leaves with one small drooping white flower shaped like a bell. The flower has 6 petals in two circles. There are green marks on the 3 small inner petals. This flower is a symbol of hope because it blooms in early spring. The flower looks like drops of snow. It grows best in zones 3 through 9. These blooms are deer resistant and can take both full sun and part sun. It is called Snowdrop (SNOH-drop).

#11. What might this flower be called?

#11. This plant has large brightly colored flowers that can be in almost any color. There can be different colors at the base of the flower. The red flowers symbolize true love while purple represents loyalty. The name of this flower may come from the Persian word for turban. This flower twists to grow towards light even in a vase. This plant can grow in zones 4 through 10. Cut flowers will keep growing. This flower is a Tulip (TOO-lip).

#12. What might this flower be called?

#12. This plant has flowers that are bright yellow. The plants can cover the ground looking like shiny gold. Do not eat this plant since all parts are poisonous. This plant grows well with Snowdrop plants. But it doesn't grow well with Crocus plants or Pansy plants.
It is
self-seeding and grows back year after year.
The plant grows in zones 4 to 7.
This plant is the Winter Aconite (WIN-tur AK-uh-night).

Parts of a Flowering Plant

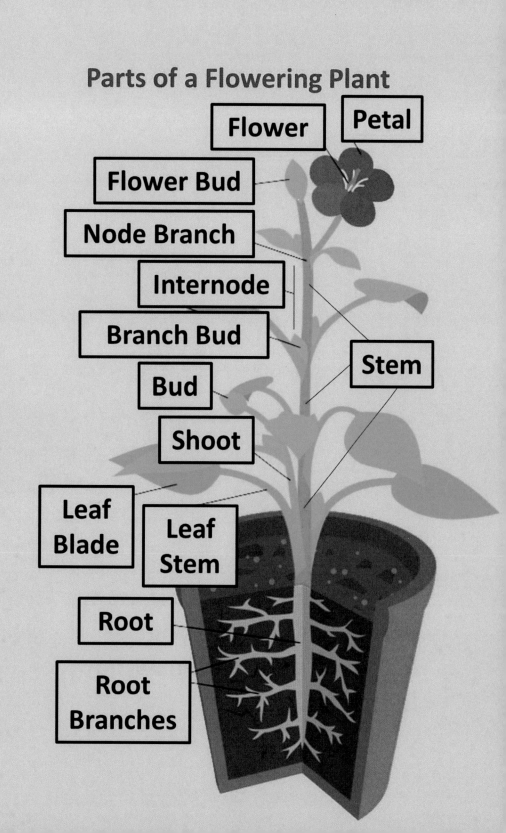

On the next page, how many Spring Flowers can you identify and describe without looking back?

Parts of a Flowering Plant

Thank you for buying this book. Dedicated to my lovely wife Sulastri and my grandchildren Mia and Kai as well as everyone who enjoys Spring Flowers.

For over forty years, I have enjoyed teaching at elementary, high school and college levels. I would love to hear from you.
Email me at richardvlinville@gmail.com

Check out my other books by searching on Kindle books for Rich Linville. Illustrations are from OpenClipArt, PixaBay, Clipart Library, Commons Wiki plus illustrations purchased from Edu-Clips.com.

45997662R00020

Made in the USA
Middletown, DE
22 May 2019